Funny Answers to Foolish Questions

Maureen Kushner

Illustrated by
Dennis Kendrick

Sterling Publishing Co., Inc.   New York

To Yippee, who always has
a funny answer for everything

Library of Congress Cataloging-in-Publication Data

Kushner, Maureen.
  Funny answers to foolish questions.

  Includes index.
  Summary: Hundreds of salty answers to more than
eighty stupid questions. For example: "Are you
leaving?" "No, I'm coming in backwards."
  1. American wit and humor. 2. Wit and humor,
Juvenile. [1. Wit and humor] I. Kendrick, Dennis, ill.
II. Title.
PN6163.K87 1987   818'.5402   87-9926
ISBN 0-8069-6442-1
ISBN 0-8069-6443-X (lib. bdg.)

ISBN 0-8069-3756-4 (pbk.)

Text copyright © 1987 by Maureen Kushner
Illustrations copyright © 1987 by Dennis Kendrick
Published by Sterling Publishing Co., Inc.
Two Park Avenue, New York, N.Y. 10016
Distributed in Canada by Oak Tree Press Ltd.
% Canadian Manda Group, P.O. Box 920, Station U
Toronto, Ontario, Canada M8Z 5P9
Distributed in the United Kingdom by Blandford Press
Link House, West Street, Poole, Dorset BH15 1LL, England
Distributed in Australia by Capricorn Ltd.
P.O. Box 665, Lane Cove, NSW 2066
Manufactured in the United States of America

CONTENTS

Chapter 1

WELCOME HOME!

Is that you?

I'm not sure. I haven't looked in the mirror lately.

I'm not sure. Ask my mother.

If it isn't, then I'm lost.

No, it's Casper, the friendly ghost.

How did you get your
new clothes so dirty?

I didn't want to get my
playclothes dirty.

I was down
in the
dumps.

My old
clothes were
dirty already.

Why does your room look like a tornado hit it?

That's not my room. It's a giant jigsaw puzzle.

You never put up the storm windows.

I was practicing search and destroy missions.

Didn't you say this house was a national disaster?

I had a brainstorm.

Did you feed
the goldfish?

Yes, I took him
out to a seafood
restaurant.

No, we ran out
of gold.

No, we ran out
of fish.

No, he was too
tired to eat from
doing all those
laps in the tank.

Are you doing
the ironing?

No, I'm just having a heated
argument with my shirt.

No, I'm just letting off steam.

No, I'm having a press conference.

No, I'm massaging the
table.

No, I'm
warming
up dinner.

13

Are you playing the piano?

No, I'm polishing my fingers.

No, I'm dusting the keys.

No, I'm playing Beethoven.

No, I'm just pushing these little black
and white things for exercise.

No, I'm taking my fingers for a walk.

No, I'm typing a letter to Bruce Springsteen.

No, the keys are making that music by themselves.

Chapter 2

FUNNY YOU SHOULD ASK.....

Are those
freckles?

No, they're a rare form of measles.

No, I recently broke out in poppy seeds.

No, they're solar batteries to power
my mind transmission.

No, that's my brain playing Follow the
Dots.

Is that a yo-yo?

No, it's just something I throw away
that keeps coming back.

No, it's a flying saucer and it's pulling
me up and down.

No, it's a Big Mac on a leash.

No, it's a basketball
and I'm doing some
slow-motion dribbling.

No, it's a very large
chocolate-covered
raisin, melting in my
hand.

Are you wearing braces?

No, I'm developing a new lock for your mouth.

No, I'm just wired.

No, this is the latest thing in tooth jewelry.

Actually, this is a nose straightener.

No, this is abstract sculpture.

No, I'm decorating my teeth for
Halloween.

No, this is leftover tinsel from the
Christmas tree.

No, this is a magnet for Tootsie Rolls.

No, these are frames for my tooth
stains.

No, I'm just trying them on for size.

No, this is a muzzle that keeps me from
biting people who ask foolish questions.

Are you waiting for the
elevator?

No, I just like to watch the doors open and close.

No, I was just standing here and they built the building around me.

No, I'm elevated enough, thanks.

No, my foot is nailed to the floor.

I wasn't—but when I met you I needed a lift.

No, I hear it's coming down with a cold.

That's an elevator? So that's why people keep going in and out!

UP

DOWN

OTHER

Are you fishing?

No, I'm just feeding the piranhas.

No, I'm installing an underwater telephone line.

No, I'm communicating with a nuclear submarine.

No, I'm just dunking a very large donut.

Are you going to school now?

No, I'm joining the army.

No, this is a command station for UFO's.

No, this is a tank. We're about to have a revolution.

My, haven't you grown?

No, you've
just gotten
shorter.

Chapter 3

KEEP
IT
CLEAN!

Why? Is one missing?

No, it was too heavy, so I took a
shower instead.

I didn't have to. Luckily, I got caught
in a carwash.

No, I just
came back
from the
cleaners.

No, I took a
prune. See
how wrinkled
I am?

No, a
swim. I
like to do
my laps in
private.

Why did you leave a ring around the bathtub?

It didn't fit my finger.

My collar already had one.

That's no ring. That's my homework.
The teacher told us to make a
rectangle.

I couldn't find a
rosy.

How come you
didn't brush your
teeth this morning?

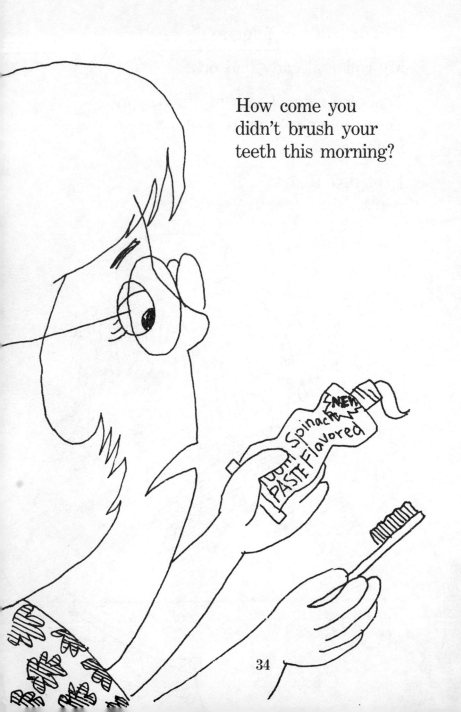

Everybody always tells me to keep my mouth shut, so I did.

I thought combing them was enough.

I didn't think you'd want to be the only one with bad breath.

I like my teeth yellow. They brighten up our boring classes.

I brushed my hair. Isn't that enough for one day?

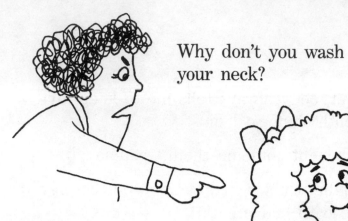

Why don't you wash
your neck?

Then it wouldn't match
the rest of me.

Why don't you wash
your face?

This isn't my face. It's
a ski mask.

Then it wouldn't match
my sneakers.

Are you sweeping your room?

No, I'm just warming up the broom for Halloween.

No, I'm tickling my pet turtle.

No, just trying to raise dust.

Why did you give the cat a bath?

The dog didn't need one.

I was checking out the water
temperature before
I washed the fish.

Did you wash the
dog?

Yes, but I couldn't get
him into the dryer.

Yes, I starched and
ironed him, too.

Chapter 4

NOT EXACTLY TEACHER'S PET

Why were you
late to school?

My nose was running and I had
to catch it.

I didn't have an American
Express card and I know I can't
leave home without one.

The car pool
ran out of
water.

The sign said
"School—Go
Slow."

I had to floss
my gerbil.

Why are you standing on the desk?

I couldn't sit through the class.

I'm practicing to be a stand-up comic.

I'm trying to overcome my fear of heights.

Because I got tired of standing on the chair.

I'm birdwatching.

I have high standards.

Is your teacher around?

No, she's a square.

Did you hurt yourself?

No, I'm getting a mummy transplant.

44

TRYOUTS FOR THE SCHOOL PLAY

TARZAN

F THE APES

Are those real muscles?

No, that's where I keep my pet turtles.

No, they're giant Twinkies in case I get hungry.

No, I always keep something up my sleeve.

Where is
your pencil?

It's home with writer's cramp.

It left. It didn't want to be #2 anymore. It wanted to be #1.

It was swallowed by the pencil sharpener.

I wanted to see if I could write with my finger.

I sharpened it, but it didn't get the point.

It died of lead poisoning.

My grandma used all my pencils for chopsticks.

Why are you
chewing gum?

Because I'm tired of chewing my nails.

I'm not chewing gum. I'm doing a
Bugs Bunny imitation.

Who, me? I'm a
food compactor
for the school
lunchroom.

I'm trying to stop
my teeth from
growing.

48

Why didn't you do your homework?

My mother is punishing me. I'm not allowed to do homework all week.

I did. I washed the dishes, made my bed, took out the garbage . . .

I would have, but my hand was in a coma.

My pen ran out and never came back.

My homework was stolen and I'm waiting for the ransom note.

49

Why didn't you go to gym?

Why should I? Jim never comes to me.

What? And work out with dumbbells?

And get athlete's foot?

Why didn't you go to football practice?

Because I don't get a kick out of it.

I already know the score.

Why were you yelling in class?

The teacher told
us to stop
whispering.

I just ate a scream cheese and
yelly sandwich.

I got stung by the spelling
bee.

My mother won't let me yell
at home.

Did you pass the note?

Oh, was that a note? I thought it was the test answers and I didn't want to look.

Why don't you use
your brain?

That would be
taking unfair
advantage of you.

It's on an extended
loan for medical
research.

I don't know how.
I lost the
instructions.

What? And stand
out from the rest of
the class?

Why don't you pay attention?

It doesn't pay me, so why should I pay it?

I can't pay attention, 'cause I don't have any money.

Because you're always telling me to be alert, and I don't even know what a Lert is.

Why don't you behave?

I do behave—badly.

Chapter 5

GO TO YOUR ROOM!

Are you walking the dog?

No, we just happen to be going in the same direction.

No, we shop at the same butcher.

No, it's walking me.

Are you feeding
the birds?

No, those two just got married and
I'm throwing rice.

No, this is a new way of planting
grass.

No, I'm leaving
gingerbread crumbs
for Hansel and Gretel.

No, I'm playing
jacks.

Are you playing baseball?

No, I use this mitt for catching butterflies.

No, I carry around this bat in case I need a toothpick.

No, this is a potholder. Would you care for some spaghetti and baseballs?

No, it's a scorcher today. I'm fanning myself.

No, this is a fly swatter. Get out of the way!

61

Are you playing the guitar?

No, I just need something to pick on.

No, I'm just stringing it along.

No, I'm filing my nails.

Are you brushing your teeth?

No, I'm mining for gold.

No, I'm washing my face from the inside.

No, I'm fishing for last night's dinner.

No, I'm polishing my tongue.

SMYLZ!

63

Are you going to take a
bath?

No, I'm just taking my rubber
duck out for a walk.

No, I don't believe in water
pollution.

No, I'm going to wallpaper the
bathtub.

No, I'm going to play water
polo with my
humpback whale.

Are you sleeping?

No, I always
look this way
when I jog.

No, I'm playing school.

No, I'm checking out
the insides of my
eyelids.

Chapter 6

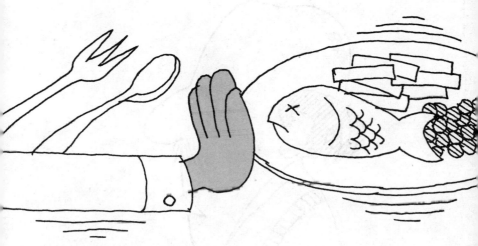

JUST LOST MY APPETITE

Why are you playing with
your food?

Is that food? I thought it was kite string.

It wouldn't be polite to play with someone else's food.

I'm not playing. This is a serious attempt to avoid food poisoning.

I wanted to save you the money it would cost for a stomach pump.

How come you're not eating your liver
when you know it's good for you?

I don't eat worms
either, but look
what they do for
birds.

One liver's enough
for me.

Liver's the wurst!

How come you're not eating your prunes?

Because they're the pits.

Because I have a date.

Because I don't give a fig.

No special raisin.

Did you eat all
the cake that
was in the
refrigerator?

Well, yes. I was counting my calories and
I needed 30,000 more to reach my goal.

Yes. You told me to put the groceries in
the refrigerator and there wasn't enough
room so I had to take out the biggest
thing and that was the cake and I knew it
would dry out so I ate it.

Cake? Is that what it was? I thought it was Irish stew!

I didn't eat it. I borrowed it because my boat needed a new anchor.

Are you eating
ice cream?

No, I keep this thing in my mouth so I
don't have to answer stupid questions.

No, this is a thermometer. If it melts, I
don't have to go to school.

No, I'm eating a
chocolate-covered
hamburger on a
stick.

Why did you start the food fight?

I didn't.
The food
started it
first.

What happened to your lunch money?

What do you think happened? It was lunch money, so I ate it.

It got eaten up by inflation.

Why were you thrown out
of the lunchroom?

My hot dog was barking.

I made cole slaw out of my Cabbage Patch doll.

I offered the cook a sample of her own cooking.

I gave my teacher a taste of my meatball and he thought I was trying to poison him.

I was fed up!

I was mud wrestling with the pot roast.

I gave the cook a pizza my mind.

Why can't you sit still?

I am sitting still. It's the rest of the room that's moving.

Chapter 7

TROUBLE!

Why did you put a snake
in your brother's bed?

It was sleepy.

Because my sister's afraid of snakes.

Because his socks keep falling down
and it was a garter snake.

The refrigerator was full.

I couldn't find a frog.

Because they're both creeps.

Why did you tell
your sister that
her skin will turn
purple when
she's 13?

Because I wanted her to have some hope for her future looks.

Won't it?

I thought she'd be happy. Purple is her favorite color.

Because she asked me.

How did you get that black eye?

I inherited it. My grandmother's a raccoon.

They didn't have any more brown ones.

I bought it at a discount store. It was made in Taiwan.

I knocked myself out doing all that homework.

I was listening to too many Knock-Knock jokes.

Why did you get an F on your test?

The kid I used to copy from moved to Siberia.

I'd like to do better but the teacher wants every word spelled the same old way every time.

Oh, I forgot to tell you. The ratings changed. F is for Fantastic.

The teacher ran out of A's.

Why didn't you show us your report card?

I haven't finished writing my will yet.

You already had too much excitement for one day.

I outgrew Show and Tell in the first grade.

And give you a nervous breakdown?

I'm not in show business.

Why did you spill chocolate all over the new white rug?

Because you threw out the old white rug.

90

Chapter 8

LOVE THAT QUESTION!

Haven't I seen you someplace before?

Maybe. Sometimes I get careless where I go.

Could be. I look like a lot of other famous people.

Did you miss me?

Why? Were you gone?

No, but I'd like to.

Afraid so, but I'll take better aim next time.

No, I'm waiting for the tide to come in.

No, I'm waiting for Michael Jackson to give me my glove back.

No, I'm waiting for *Rocky XVIII* to come out.

No, I'm waiting for Stevie Wonder to perform another miracle.

How come you didn't call me like you said you would?

I called and called, but you didn't answer, so I threw out the megaphone.

The phone was tied up and I didn't have a scissors.

I got hung up.

E.T. used my quarter to phone home.

Call you what?

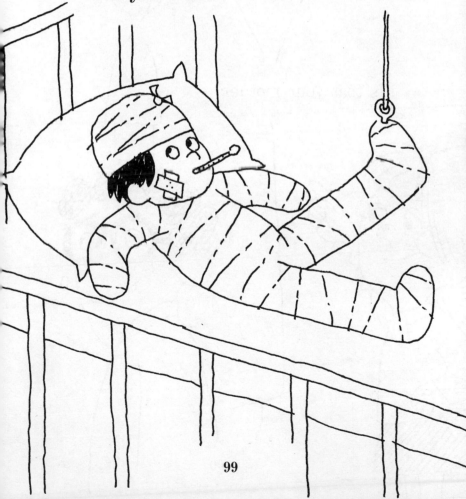

Is that your mother?

No, it's my father. My mother has shorter hair.

No, that's Snow White, and I'm one of the seven dwarfs.

No, it's just some strange lady I go to see when I want to be criticized, scolded and humiliated.

Ask her. When it happened I was too young to remember.

No, she's from the Youth Employment Office and she hired me to be her child for the day.

TICKET

TICKET BUYERS LINE

No, it's my girlfriend. I go for older women.

SLIME STRIKES BACK!

Now Showing

NO PASSES

Are you mad at me?

No, my hands are just trying your neck out for size.

No, I always froth at the mouth.

No, crimson is my natural complexion color.

Chapter 9

YOU ASKED
FOR IT!

Would you like a piece of my mind?

No, thank you, enough has been broken off already.

Better not. You can't spare it.

No, we don't accept defective merchandise.

No, but maybe another piece of pie?

How stupid do you think I am?

Not as stupid as you look.

I never said you were stupid,
but I'd like to use your head
for my rock collection.

How many times have I told you not to
do that?

I don't know. I haven't
learned to count
that high yet.

Who do you think you're talking

How many guesses do I get?

I don't know.
What's your name?

Your guess
is as good
as mine.

Why don't you act your age?

I'm a kid, not an actor.

I gave up acting
lessons for karate.

Do you think I'm a perfect idiot?

Nobody is perfect.

No, a defective one.

No, but I wish you were a perfect stranger.

No, but you do a great imitation.

Do you have a cold?

No, this is actually an extremely contagious form of the plague.

No, I always use my nose to water the lawn.

No, I'm warming up for the Boston Nose-Running Marathon.

Will you help me out?

If you promise to stay out.

Delighted! Which way did you come in?

Did you cut
your hair?

No, I had my ears
lowered.

No, I got them all
cut.

No, I melted the
ends off.

No, I washed my
hair in hot water
and it shrunk.

What time is it?

Time for you to get a new watch.

Same as yesterday, only a day later.

Time for you to get your act together and take it on the road.

May I ask a question?

You just did!

Chapter 10

GOING BANANAS

Was that your foot?

It's all right. I still have one left.

It's okay. I had two left feet anyway.

I don't know. I'll try matching it when I get back from the hospital.

It's okay. I only walk on the bottom.

Why are you crawling on the ground?

I wanted to see the floor show.

So we could see eye-to-eye.

I'm not crawling. I'm drilling for oil.

I've always been fascinated by the underworld.

I'm not crawling on the ground. It's dinnertime and I'm grazing.

Why do you bite your nails?

Is there something else you'd rather see me bite?

I only eat organic foods.

Why? Would you like me to bite someone else's nails?

I like to keep my snacks handy.

Because hammers are too big to fit in my mouth.

I don't bite my nails. I file my teeth.

Why are you sticking out your tongue?

It doesn't fit in my mouth.

I'm trying to see if it's raining.

I'm not sticking it out. My lips are receding.

I'm catching flies for my science experiment.

I wanted to see what pollution tastes like.

Is that your swimming pool?

No, it's a birdbath for my brontosaurus.

No, it's a chlorine beach.

No, it's a training school for rubber ducks.

No, it's an aquarium for my pet shark.

No, it's a footbath for the Jolly Green Giant.

No, we struck oil.

Why were you called into the principal's office?

He wanted my recipe for spitballs.

I was inviting him to our class riot.

Because of illness. The teacher got sick of me.

To get first prize in the talking marathon.

Is that your guinea pig?

No, it's a ham sandwich in fuzzy bread.

No, it's a miniature elephant.

No, it's a ferocious guard dog in disguise.

Why are you wasting your time reading that book?

I'm not. I stopped reading on page 11.

Foolish Question Checklist
(and Index)